THINGS I NEVER KNEW:

THERE IS SOMETHING SINISTER TO IT

THINGS I NEVER KNEW: THERE IS SOMETHING SINISTER TO IT

AARON QUINN

WALNUT STREET
—PUBLISHING—

ISBN 978-1-7342750-5-6

Walnut Street Publishing
1645 S Holtzclaw Ave
Chattanooga, TN 37404

TO THE SIDE STREET WANDERERS, MAD HATTER POETS, ROCK-IN-THE-JAW PAINTERS, AND FENCE-JUMPING CREATIVES- THIS IS FOR YOU. I DO NOT EXIST WITHOUT YOUR INSPIRATION.

LET US SMASH SOMETHING AND MOSH THROUGH THIS COLLECTION TOGETHER. HOPEFULLY, YOU WILL FIND YOURSELF SOMEWHERE IN THESE LINES.

YELLOW MOTH

Windchimes and Counter Culture coffee
on the back porch this morning.
We watched the yellow moth eat
the hemlock leaf-
     a snapshot of my deepest held belief:

Joy-
     a singularity
     a meta.

You pointed at a tree
alone in the neighbor's field
with limbs gangly like witches' fingers.
but the moth's brown speckled wings possessed my eyes.

A glass can only spill what it contains,
and joy comes from the cloudy glass:
     tell me all your thoughts,
     I say as the moth eats away.

I do not know, damnit, I do not know,
you shout, jovially shaking your fist at
the swelling clouds.

Only a fool thinks he knows in all
but a wise man knows in part-
the universe can expand when
we do not know,

The gyre might spin, but love, I like
your steady eyes that make me emotionally
 naked in your sight
     Would you hand me a leaf Eve?

1

The yellow moth flits its wings but stays.
as we shoot buckshot memories
in our rotting chairs:

Fooly Cooly at four AM
　　　　that snaps me back
to gravel crunching, middle-of-the-road walking,
before our time, but then you remind me of
Huntsville bookshop hunting,
and Faulkner grave handholding.

I chatter about lavender lattes,
clover Meade, and back pocket Freud at weddings

You bring us blackberry jam and artisan bread.
Then reclaimed your Star Mountain dreams asking:
Do you think I am a wounded bird with
clipped wings? Or am I a hologram?

The loud cymbals clashing out of
your confusion made you strum
your guitar.

　　　　　All those moments gone
　　　　　but the moth's wings ignored the wind.

I close my eyes, you light birch and sandalwood
and we go silent to admire the beauty of the moth-bites
in the leaf:

and with the coffee cup emptying
those bites are my deepest-held belief.

STILL A GRAPE

A grape turned into wine is still a grape,
just like an assault turned into art is still an assault.

3

IF THUNDER SCARES A SLEEPING CAT, WHAT DOES IT DO TO A WELCOME MAT?

a human remains out there- not in here.

The rain whips sideways
smashing against the freshly cleaned four-paned windows.
Gentle Thursday yawned yellow and bright,
now roars grumpy and grey,
water pools on the highway.

a human remains out there
tormented by the wind's anger and lightning's wrath.

4

IF WE DID NOT HAVE FINGERPRINTS, MAYBE YOUR GHOST WOULD LEAVE

There is a thumbprint on the mirror—
someone has been here before.

TWERKING LEADS TO ARTHRITIS OF THE HIPS AND I THINK ARMADILLOS WOULD MAKE A KILLER PET

It might take a steady hand to navigate the choppy waters
of death's sneering pursuit, but I do better with a frown
that fits perfectly like auspicious cufflinks worn during august
bonfires, burning red to signify that something is already dead.
There is dignity in the whiskey slipping sideways
out of my mouth when I laugh at satellite sights and
grandeur in the dance of living off my forfeits,
seeking inclusion, not exclusion
with pennies in the blue blown bowl on the dresser,
and dime-sized words on my tongue, curlicued
and unintelligent thoughts dressed up nicely by borrowed diction-
          all hail the Chumbscrubber.
She said catawampus, now the ta wamp sounds good
when connected to thoughts that go bump in the night.
Fright not from the shadows, but the seen in my wonderment eyes
that makes it seem that death's flirtation fancys
a palaver with the devil in me.
Do I worship Jesus because he has a death fetish like me-
suffered in all ways- meet me at high noon gunslinger,
I have emotions to misunderstand!- and a gospel to spread, but I
first have to understand how to doubt enough to back into belief.
I use every person as a mirror on the wall-
halfway to being honest until someone else's reflection looks better.
I hate understanding Demogorgon and Hobbits more
than the words that come from the Pinegrove-inspired
Parties where everything is relevant but my perspective.

My mother made me autistic, not white- that muddles and befuddles
as the bully from when I was four still has a rhythm in my head.
The taste of Amen and a good stout heals-
His yoke is easy- but how do I forget that
I had my first drink three weeks in the womb
          and dreamt of the tomb ever since.

NO ONE WILL HEAR THE SOUND IF WE CRACK THE FURY OF BEING SEEN

Seashells from the shores
by the bedside in a borrowed jar.
We slept in the silence
of May, feeling brand new.
Woke and walked where dandelion
petals dropped at our feet,

Your hair danced as we went
down where the grass grows.
Strawberries picked
without need for shoes,
red stained fingers
pushed away the weeds watching
for garden snakes

      until we saw the hidden path and you
      followed behind, hoping no one would hear our sound.

BLOWING DANDELIONS

Coyotes cackle between blowing dandelions,
yellow eyes watching coyly
as eleven turns to the witching hour.

FOUND A PICTURE OF YOU

This morning, I found a picture of you
hidden in a wooden grape crate.
Your eyes stared back, lost in a Sistine Chapel gaze-
     Catholic raised, Baptist regret.

The ducks chitchatted around the scorched fire pit earth,
their blathering chatter real-
but I failed to hear your voice looking back at me.

Sober stillness hung like a vaulted ceiling,
a touch of flu with cinnamon tea ran through-
a vortex of steeped sadness,
for years you hid away in the crate,
but this morning, I found a picture of you-

The family never speaks your name.
They have lost your recipes-
Granny, are we already through with you?
Did we die, too?

Eden was not mine, but the picture is.
I wonder what we did with your coffee mug.
Body incinerated; bridges destroyed:
How tall was our Christmas tree?

I found a picture of you, and now I
single hand hold it like a carcinogenic noir memoir-
your frown robs the hues from the fading memory
as times tyranny distills the sound of your laugh.

If I hold my breath until blue, I stand like you,
inching closer to being near: Dread dear,
it has all been dread since your hospice bed:

but today I found a picture of you
looking back, pleading
for us not to be dead, too.

NIGHTSTAND MEMORIES, RELIGIOUS REGRETS PUT ON SERRETTE LETTERS

With familiar handwriting,

      the note sat on her mother's nightstand:

I was not born in sin,
neither were you,
tell Daddy goodbye.

She left in an ironed blouse
with Ohio on her mind-

      the nightstand refused to leave,
      but she could never stay.

CAST-IRON SIMPLICITY IN A BICKERING WORLD

Quite hours turn to years.
Kettles whistling. Cured cast-iron.
Time tamed by the minute moments:
hummingbird chirps, purple lilac fields picked.

Hot tea and lemon shaving mornings
melt away into soft silver moon shards
reflecting off brown-stained rocking chairs.

THEN THERE WERE RIPPLES

There were no ripples in the pond before
the pontoon boat disturbed the peace.
Safety. Natural. Negation.
Largemouth bass swam without threat,
the snapping turtles basked on a rock.
Then the hook snared the water.
Scattered. Unsafe. Negation.
There were no ripples until there were
all to honor when man decided
to make creation after his own image.

KYOCHIKUTO

The cat creeps on the edge of the crabgrass,
no bomb for it to recall,
>   but the nuclear shadow still veils my sight as I watch him

creep,
>   creep,
>   creep.

Claws stay hidden until the grass is too deep,
like scars from the explosion-
choke the fumes, choke the radiation,
choke until I realize that the bomb
>   sits on my tongue.

We bury the sins of our parents
as though holy-
>   status, not action-

Creator denied
with nuclear halos
creating radiation flowers,
>   they were us, they were me,
>   how can the bomb cease to be?

I ally with the destruction when ignoring the widow,
and hold the munition when blind ambition
cherishes belletristic heirlooms over
acknowledging earth's wounds.

Dots of red oleanders remained, so did the stain-
the almond scent could not cover destruction's tattoos.

It has come to this,
did they think of the hibiscus?

do I?

Is there a bomb in my pupil to remove?
Fat Man, then Little Boy dispersed-
names given, names robbed-

Mothers stood at the cradle
as pilots watched the bombs fall:
there were humans below.

The reverberation warbles in my heart
when I ignore the swelling undertow
that pulls me into the underbelly that
justified the bomb's hatch opening-
        prayers for survivors never resurrected
        the bodies of the humans below.

Bombastic bombardment
the arm of Mars gluttonly stretches as the bombs fall
to scoop out the
guts of humanity with
crimson red in his eyes-

        what color are mine?

TOMATO SEED DEPTH AND OPTIMUS PRIME'S DEATH
BROUGHT MATURITY AND HEAPS OF TRAUMA

Bosom baby, southern born, birthed near
bruised trees where the tobacco leaves hung.

Given sweet corn summers with river jumping boys.

Then, backwoods winter with deer
being chopped down by rifle wishes.

The Lord's water washed away adolescence,
baptized words were bloodied by vulgar desperation.

Grandpa put the tomato a thumbprint deep-
a seed planted by a heavy hand never reaches maturity.

Forever a Southern child- Grandpa trusted me enough to
live in the freedom of a properly planted tomato seed.

LISTEN, I CARE LIKE A MAGNET STUCK TO A SINKING SHIP

An iron ship of desperation
holding an origami heart-
paper thin and constructed by another hand-
there is no drowning when pride buoys
perception.

How do I slouch toward Jerusalem when
banks and government buildings
cover up the hills from where my help comes?

I LIVE A NO TACO LEFT BEHIND TYPE OF LIFE WITH HOT SAUCE SHOTS AND BREATH MINT DESSERTS

Winding wanders through rockslides
and rough times, ducking fallen powerlines, and tornado debris.
Hip-clipped carabiner, the hydro flask flailed against our
thighs and yellow bamboo yoga mats sat easily against
our worn-out backpacks.

The wine clattered joyfully as
we hopped from rock to bridge.
Gee Creek streams scattered about,
we waded through the day without our shoes,
married to pine sap-sticky ring fingers and lingering silence.

The water bloomed in our ears
as the cave mouth moused about
the peripheral of our fear.

The current pooled around our weightless heads.
Sugar sweet, flirtation meek-
we memorized the skylines, not wanting to
miss the chattering waterfall
orate freedom while rubbing
boulders bald as the fire smoldered with a
reservoir of tortured limericks.

PATTERING FEET

A song sparrow stretches her wings between
harmonizing with the squirrels' pattering feet.
To be the sparrow is to be one that flies to
what is ahead, forgetting what is already behind.

DECLUTTER THE TABLE OR ADMIT CHAOS IS THE CAKE OF THE DAY

Does an enlightened person know they are?
If humility is part of it, then
how does one climb the heights to
accept they have more knowledge
than the unenlightened?
Should I even want to be enlightened?
Or should I want to be decluttered?

SOMETIMES LESS IS MORE BUT THERE IS NO ROOM TO TALK ABOUT MARBLES IN SHORT TITLES

A stone skipping over water
propagates ripples,
and both stone and water embrace
the disruptive collision.

ROLLERBLADING WITH A MACHETE ON A COBBLED ROAD AND EATING SUSHI OFF A BATHROOM FLOOR SEEM LIKE BAD IDEAS WHEN I STILL HAVE NOT SWAM WITH THE MANATEES

I do not want the day, give me the night.

The bustling streets become lethargic,
all is but a shadow.
Audacious insolence douses anxiety
with gasoline passion.

Every blue morning glory must step
aside for the chaos of the night-
I thank ye, for the sacrifice.

To destroy is to reimagine with fresh eyes.
Out of chaos comes creation-
my mania is chaos, too-
give me the muddled inspiration of night
not the clear definition of day.

There is no room for slanted grey depression words
to thrive when others can see the blight-
the locust swarms are where my art is found.
it might be a long way down, but the
night sky never promised a way back-

Pass the empty cup, smash the glass.
Beauty blooms in the destruction of order-
that, too, is creation.
I do not want the day. Give me the night.

Chaos found a way to create sheets of discomfort
with cold backs turned to opposite doors
- jah werx.

Open the grave, wipe the cobwebs,
waltz with the silent murderer-
capitalism is the true mediocrity.

The smog of business lunches
thinly veils my ravenous need for everything all at once-
turning my mind's eye into a basket full of holes.

Safety is an illusion
   - chaos in desire, cosmos in creating.

Perpetually jealous of forgotten times when streams
shattered the demands of the day- smash, I say, just smash
and dash until the railroad tracks end.

Them are the breaks kid,
remembrance is a river that flows best at night-
   haunted landscapes lingering turn water into wine-
Ouija board dreams are more fun when
running away from broken things.

Social implications are not the lot I want to roll.
A torn shirt is no good in a blizzard,
but chaos, babe, I just need the chills of chaos
to survive.

A frozen rose, fevered and blistered,
I listen for a door I cannot find:

I do not want the day, give me the night.

SILENCE IS A GRACE

Nature does not need to be loud to rebel.

I had to kill your mom
without calling you mother.

I used to pray for you
from morning to noon.
My fat tongue grieving
before being weened.

Granny had to die in my mind
to understand my bastard liturgy
made me your least favorite decision.

Malted liquor tasted better
than eight-hour trips
to see your confused progeny.

My dog ate my whitish-grey bunny and still
had more compassion than your womb.

What do you do? Can your memory
not be through?

No longer incubator, never mother,
only flawed human.

Stranger wake,
I need you to wake.

walk out of your grave
because I now know what to say.

MUDDY CLAY BANKS LEAD TO WHITE SHOE HOMICIDE

The car sits miles out of sight
far away from where the willows catch the brisk wind-
one set of footprints walking toward the trail.
.

All feels strange on the muddy clay banks
while waiting, listening
to the lack of muffler rumbles

            and being panged by lavender evening scents.

A single shadow refracts off the water
crinkled, unrecognizable.
Whip-poor-wills chirp in the early morning cool,
they collide ugly with absence
like a cat-of-nine-tails is tangled around their notes.

My remorse-shrunken spine elongates
over river rocks while I embalm the memory
of two shadows sliding down
once-familiar mocha walls where goodbye's lips
poured into time's infant hand.

MOON PIES THREE TIMES A DAY MIGHT SEEM LIKE A BAD MEAL PLAN UNTIL YOU REALIZE LIFE IS ALL ENTROPY AND TOILET PAPER THEN ONE WATCHES THE WEATHER CHANNEL FOR FUN- KERCHUNK

The good life is not fitted for me.
I am consumed by wanting to
live at the bottom of a rogue wave with
unhinged rattlesnake jaws stuck trying to find oxygen.
My skin feels like a garment holding a couple's outdated desire-
if they could leave, why should I not mirror those who wear buttons
for eyes?

       Alone is not suicide, but to be surrounded is to die-
that is not the wave- it is fate-
so I pawn scratched-record-solitude for death by a thousand voices-
icy ick, life never fit like a shoe-

jealous longing elucidates poetry more than obedient death-

Suicidal weeks, bursting joy days- there is no between-
believe me, I usually lie- I smiled falling out the Ocoee raft-
dreams started coming true then two
hands ripped me up without consent.

Rent tore the afternoons from the banana yellow plastic-
there is no romance to be had in alarm clock reminders.

Apathy leading to sympathetic views of the mundane-
that is true regret- there is always so much blood to see.
Give me the mistakes, all the mistakes,
they let me know I am not afraid to bleed.

Dislocate the shoulder, pop the joint, there
ain't enough junk up the nose to convince me
to get a new suit lobotomy-
weekly grief with every timeclock kerchunk,

sycophantic symphonies, maybe I was born to perform.

I am a sunken ship, always a sunken ship, and a sunken ship
knows how to successfully drown-
Pull me under, inundate me with saltwater lullabies and
hasty goodbyes- this is the wave.

Resistance is prophetic in a Socratic not giving-a-damn type of way.

Smokey pines and burning pipes,
there is a place already been and a place
one wishes to be- what good is mental health if I drown alone?

I once found one that properly knew how to drown-
take my hand- the dust that lies in her lies in me.

Cold drizzle freely dripped between crate slats as
we shivered outside- a flood can start with a simple mist.
No one can touch the paint smudge,
it pulls me further under the wave-
A staggering dove, stammering tongue-
quick quips about nights traveled shoeless crossing yellow lines
tangling through a long twine of highway
in her state-to-state stories will always be my preferred baptism-
a brushstroke controlled is a brushstroke reduced.

                    -but then there were none-

Whispers of autumn hair and independent stares
were the remains of the day.

Chattanooga never felt like home, Bean Station neither
they could never be the rogue wave and
life is better when there is enough drowning to share.

BROKEN RECORD LULLABY

Blandly walking along railroad ties
ripping up rapture tracks with fading ink-
socially relevant shadow hoppers
waiting to see if we are so American
or something similar to a broken record lullaby.

SHOTGUN LUCK AND BUCKSHOT HOLES

Falls passed on the eastside mountain slopes,
salty deer jerky in pocket,
searching for red ginseng berries-
nature given, government regulated.

Squirrel stew and sweet cornbread after
hoping the finds can pay the fines
for transporting corn whiskey with headlights off
through washed-out gravel roads.

Shotgun luck and buckshot holes
mix with outhouse refurbished lumber used to
build a barn in a weekend.

Fireball candy red tomatoes drop from the vine-
the storms come, the storms go
displacing all Bean Station knows-
marriages and gardens, too.

DESTROY THE DAM, MA'AM BEFORE THEY SEE WE ARE FREE

We have a problem with their shoes and their views-
    maybe the illusion is through-
conceit in opinion, lack of empathy in silence.

Our souls are nostalgic with should have been there
Natty Ice swigs.

Do you know the sound of a heart?
Railroad stakes and squealing brakes gave love
diction outside of addiction rooms
and thuddings from broom handles.
Escaping escapades while we listened to the sound of our hearts-
the beating of reciprocation from sycophantic junkies,
    prophetic in a want-to-be way.

Destroy the dam, the pressure is building
destroy the dam, our my mind is cracking
destroy the dam so the flood can come through.

FUTURE CORPSES

We lay as future corpses
destined to worm out of sight
listening to the whispering rain

       like it is gossip.

Limbs screech against the window-
tornado memories cripple your
ability to stay still.

Old cabin porches live in me
kinetic, stasis- expanding, retracting-
I know and forget you all the same.

There will be nights the coming dew-bent flowers are pleasant-
but life must emerge from sunken cheek stories
of creek smores for decay to go away.

Two currents charge our disheveled thoughts - joy/despair
       both a straightjacket.
They are mine, they are yours,
they are by our side on every streetcorner,
when we lay as future corpses.
.

Even when my heart is not true,
it is still real, trapping me in a soft brain stupor.
       Masks fit nicely when the heart hides,
       pass the flask to share.

All questions muddle
next to your mottled skin, wondering if the dancing
light is a talisman of our shame.

Montages of erotic sabbaths
and chip fingernail polish.
- a libation to a god we wish to know-
        encounter, not a thought.

I am/I must be,
unwanted dichotomy
        there then, here now, where tomorrow?

Crawl, crawl, crawl back into the womb-
mother or tomb,
the tune blares, broken glass expectations
cut the eyes out of dopamine dreams
        as we lay as future corpses
        refusing to accept love's sabbath rest.

TRESPASSER

Cathead biscuits, burnt gravy, and
cast iron sizzling sausage-

Sunday breakfast and slow hammock
afternoons invited me to come home

beyond the no trespassing sign-
        but they call me trespasser

while crossing 81 out of Knoxville into Blaine-
the shame of not being and being all the same.

SLOW

Sometimes I need the day to slow
to a screeching halt
allowing me to watch the ducks waddle and
listen to the crying cats.

IDOL OF MY IMAGINATION

If I do not doubt, then God is an idol
of my imagination.

If I do doubt, I come to the edge of
reason without knowing if I am
foolish or faithful.

To know all- make myself god.
To doubt- to distrust the pastor's surety
of their god.

There is a crevice between some
and all, faith asks that I define
the distance by saying I know
nothing at all.

THERE IS A ME YOU LOVED IN THE DARK

Thirty-five cents and fairyland on Walnut Street Bridge-
a reality, a caricature- seen by some,
experienced by us in the cool tiled kitchen with the
version of reality we presented while you put
grass-fed butter in fair trade coffee.
We talked about bones and rusted things and sinking stones:
that suited us just fine-

> knowing there is a me you loved in the dark-

and found joy in gasps and grimaces-
broken vases holding flowers planted by our parents.

Chattanooga, our beacon.

Moving boxes, your weapon-
> to go or to stay- your smile never gave away
which shoes you wore today-
an iridescent smile or mangled emotion-
look at the me you love in the dark.

You stepped through the threshold every night
like a lady pregnant with unborn light then flickering candles
brought incantations and distant stares you only
shared with the me you loved in the dark.

> Semantics waited in the shadows to see if the pithy
> or our connection won the day.

You were there, a sure mast to guide through the waves.
What comes first: misery or honesty?
California stayed out west, and Bean Station
stayed tucked in between pages
not knowing if we wanted them to turn-

        the joy was in the gasps, not the gaps
        between crossing bridges that led to a future.

Obsidian thoughts spewed
in the hue of magnetic emotional storms,
eruptions from oceanic wells of confusion,
a millennium of questions in a teacup of life-
you macheted your own trail,
leaving the snakes in the weeds
where sinking stones sit unencumbered by complicated things-

        and there you left me, too, with no shoes

destined to wait until another orated their thoughts
on skulls and rusted things like they could
see to the bones when looking at the me you loved in the dark.

IF THE NIGHT BELONGS TO LOVERS THEN I LOOKS LIKE I AM GOING HOME NIGHTLESS

Maroon warmth,
mixed with shards of broken words
ricochet off scars.

An arm comes out of the moon
as slinks into the sheets
drain her color
beneath the clattering fan.

Terror's underbelly
covers the night
so we can unify
in our mutual disgust
for tomorrow's boredom.

In no time, we will unfurl
like a ribbon revealing
the surprise of a present
and the day will seem
like a punishment
for an undisclosed sin.

MY SKIN, TOO

Skewered tree limbs and icicle-dripping sounds.
Brisk wintery nights blow against fragile bones.

Snowflakes fall all too clear-
      I am desperate for color and warmth.
      Is this a joke? Why does this feel like a joke?

Ravenous cabin fever.
            Mental apathy.

Why can I not see the way out?

Inside a slow boiling pot-
breath white in the air.

      It looks profane,

while my words hang in the thick winter humidity.

Where is the sun?

      Why is the sky grey?

      My skin, too?

Nature needs a rest- maybe it is time for life's sabbath,
but life cannot be planted in frozen ground.

POPS RAN AWAY, SO RETIRE THAT NAME

They want me to be a father-
surely you know it is the Father's will:
Swallow or choke, just consume that pill, white man-
a proper Christian male must spread their seed:
My Grandpa- father.
My father- a walking casket.
Unsure I know how to be like either:
a bell jar works better as a cover, not a guide.

THERE IS A REALITY WHERE TRANSFORMERS ARE HUMAN, AND WE ARE THE MACHINES

One night, the rickety logs of the rented
cabin shook from the storm-
scattered leaves and sideways rocking chairs
proved it was not in my head.

    On another,
I imagined the chirping was a black rook
chipping at the branches not knocked off by the wind-
    this was all in my head.

During both her tarot card hands rested on my arm-
    were they ever real?

Then she went away.
A black lake is assumed to have a bottom, but one never
knows unless they are brave enough to drown.
    How far down can one see the moon shards?

Then she returned, and we stood on the
porch picking cotton candy clouds
out of the sky before they disappeared behind Lookout Mountain-
    maybe it was all in my head- black rook thoughts in Tennessee
summer haze.

Blueberry bushes stained her plucking fingers
under galaxies drifting away-
    shadows of a migraine pulled against my will.
She always migrated to her next inspiration-
for a day, a week, sometimes more.

Entropy, friends, it is all entropy until decay wins-
    shotgun beginnings, tombstone finishes.

Did she hear the train shake the window

or feel my scream hidden in the sounds?
    maybe it was all supposed to be in my head-
black rook hope imagined is worth more than
decaying dandelions in the hand.

Each time, she pointed at a crack in the bark
a million branches swayed in her eyes,
some Georgia pines and other Alabama oaks-
and I always wished to see a black rook land on each one.

Is it better to love a real person or the one in my head?
Even black holes disappear, but the branches in her eyes
never faded- at least, I imagined they stay.

.

Dull ruinous neutrality dissipated when I felt like an
abstraction, not a whole, as her hag hand
gripped the chair, and I wondered if she was really there-
    I think all moments might be made up in my head.
Liquid sunsets on every branch guided her through the storms.

The world started with a fire and
desire viciously separates when it presents as a glycerine
gumdrop- a thornbush pedagogy of patience and acceptance-
but there is a reality where the black rook
sitting on the branch was not just in my head-

    Entropy, she said, it is all entropy unless I love something
that is real instead of the one decaying in my head-

Maker's Mark shots be damned, will I be okay if
she always remains the chirping rook in my head.

FOG-COVERED CHATTANOOGA, DECONSTRUCTION COVERED COFFEE

Broken-down cars lost on the street.
Buggies pushed down the sidewalk
like society rushed away from them.
Strawberry foam cappuccino and
ink plots through the paper-
June humidity sticks against table slats.
Fog covers Lookout Mountain

as though God
        waits for a palaver.

STOP SPYING ON THE EASTER EGGS, THEY WILL BE GONE TOMORROW

All art is an act of voyeurism, so
I hide you like an easter egg safely
in the lines where no one will know your name
or the color of your eyes.

STRANGER

A shadow always returns for the
stranger if they patiently wait long enough
under a buckeye-dropping tree.

A CLOWN THAT WEARS A RED NOSE HAS CLEAN STYLE, BABE

I once met a man who was not afraid to bleed
wearing a Dropkick Murphy's shirt
and funeral grey pants- he existed in a place stuck
between the warmth of dawn and the darkness of
overindulgence, a fever dream that made me
hallucinate about emotional freedom.

His cold, stoic eyes found joy in saying:
life is, at best, a longshot bet, you
are going to drop dead, accept it, and
smash some trashcans; that is the only
appropriate way to live.

I dared care where he slept, with a twitching snowy nose
he asked if a clown has a balloon to sleep in
then turned his back on me and screamed off the bridge
hoping a passing boat would catch his drift when he proclaimed
that he believed in exactly nothing:
That ain't true kid, I believe in too much,
but never tell anyone, or I will make you believe in bleeding.

Not a day went by without him walking through how
heartbreak was the splendor of love-
one must exist for the other to thrive:
laconic prayers and long soliloquies always melted the day-

I cannot forget the thick forgiveness woven in his voice.

When I asked who he prayed to, he would put a handful of dirt
on my palm and say I could find his god in the pile
not in a synthetic operation of building an identity

On the days I walked up to him while he was rolling,
he would flick his

zippo then start like he had never spoken before with the same
disclaimer:

Listen I never shot a Joan,
but I aimed for plenty of apples-
Puff the dragon, spit some fires, and fluff buffed pillows,
because there is no fun if everyone agrees in your views-

His freedom was not one I knew how to walk in.

Yellow nails scratching jaundice pleasant theories he looked
at others like love was a straightjacket he desired, constantly
proclaiming that when a man falls in love, he falls into a pit
to construct an edifice of consumption.

He would push me to rush to let go,
to find out how to live like a transmutation of energy to destruction-

Listen, kid, life is dust to destruction- if a man ever
says dust-to-dust, then he is afraid to lose it all and
one cannot truly be free until they smash the pearl and burn the
field.
A pipe has to contain fire to smoke,
the ground can crack and that serves it just fine,
but a cracking window lets in the cold.

On and on he went, spewing then listening to the world
I was not free enough to see until
he drifted off to believing in nothing again with
a piss water 40 in his hand
and a grin that confirmed there was only depression ahead.

His church was the arms of another, always prepared to bleed,
more ready to lose faith in himself- all praise be, damn the man, and
damn the one that rather raise a fence instead of a fist-

double wides and two-for-one bud lights were his kryptonite on
Mondays
but he needed whisky burning his gums by Saturday-

The man knew, somehow the man
always knew that he was the wasteland
and the current love was his whimper.

I once knew a man who was not afraid to bleed
but was brave enough to leave me with a handshake and a note
he scribbled on the back of someone's parking ticket:

To hell with bohemianism and imposed eccentricity,
ride the wave down to your mausoleum before you crash
into the guardrails of needing to be an odd songbird-
it is not about being different, it is about being free
and true to your instinctive individuality.

Now, as I drive carefully down I-75, I wonder if the guardrails
are a guide or a metaphor for how I still have not walked with his
freedom.

STEP ONE, DO NOT QUESTION, STEP TWO, GIVE YOUR IDENTITY, STEP THREE, TRULY BE ALL YOU CAN BE

Out of step ants marching to
avoid the rising tide of time,
even graves get washed over by the flood.

We were not born in sin-
if we do not say yes to now
then our fear will be what life is about-
       time waits for none but accuses us of our forfeits.

Put on your favorite shoes,
I will fit into dime-size words
to mask my stuttering insecurity
then we will go dancing as though flood
waits another day.

All void, all a mystery,
       the pictures on your phone say we were together yesterday
but where has yesterday gone if I cannot touch
your hand while you wore that smile?

WRAP MY BODY IN A MUSHROOM SUIT AND CALL IT A DAY

Even the briars are gentle
after I kiss your forehead
to leave for Laurel Lake
where Goya's paintings permeate
as his hand strikes against
every splintered piece of bark-

black spider, orange leaf
to the wild, I must go.
when chaos charges with horns drawn.

Brawny pines never question
their own autonomy-

       Nature is never too much
       or not enough,

it just is and to be makes
me dread the cruelty
when the silence ends
and I succumb to someone
else's definition of responsibility

though they will not stand
by my body wrapped in a mushroom suit
at the bottom of a holler with quarters over my eyes
nor can they find an answer to what is why.

TRANSIENT

Even a bee looks transient
on their flight with pollen taken
from in-bloom wildflowers dressed
in blue and purple suits
until they arrive to give generously
to Silver Queen cornstalks that
pillowing steps deer will eat
while the sun-scorched farmer sleeps.

DARK MOTHER

Confused looks out the window
became paperweight questions never answered.

You once spoke to the flowers,
   at least I assume.
Struggles consumed and exhumed
time and again- Mother, please
explain why your tragedy is still with me?

Klonopin promises while holding
corded phones in doublewides.
Double-fried, you lied, you had to lie to hide
after you wedded errors and chased
catatonic doldrums to become a numb vase.

Greenslick raincoat in the doorway
with a packed suitcase, I was too short to
see out the window- seven and ready for a mother
with purple soda pop stained cheeks-
   who were you
   but a dark mother
and the monster that hid in me-
I never claimed I was brave.

Did you wear nail polish
or mash the skins with the potatoes?

Time waned, faces dissipated without a name,
soft air, cobbled sidewalks,
poof gone, pursuing natures roof-
   not you, you dare not be through-
   memory like a fire stain.

Amber honey knifed thinly through

peanut butter sandwiches held
by my fat fingers were never made by your hand.
No muddy river baptism or mother's day-

did my face terrify?-

I wish I could claim to be brave.

Sixteen with vengeful forgiveness
guiding my terrified tongue,
I hung up, not knowing where
you were- just not near, my dark mother.

You never passed through the valley
to sit idly and watch the deer
eat in the hayfield-
you had so much hurt to give-
the darkness shows I still grieve,
addling my fidelity to the present.

You were alive and now are a fish
decoupaging my steps into a barbwire collage
of all that remains

Time makes the cracks hard to caulk back together-
your absence gave and gave and gave,
then you were forever gone. Mother, I
still do not know where you are
now that the wind has scattered your ashen remains-

and I still lack the strength to say that I am brave.

THIS PHOTO DOES NOT BELONG TO US- STEVE MCCURRY SHOULD BE ARRESTED FOR ASSAULT

Burn the photo, burn the magazine,
her piercing eyes are not consent-
neither was her 10-year-old refugee body.

Held captive because of a greedy American lens,
exploited when she did not have much choice
and that was good enough for artistic prestige
while the 10-year-old turned 30 and still had to flee.

She was a pressured child.
He was an artistic man.

Why did he take money for the photo
but never rescue her from Pakistan?

Consent
Consent
Consent

Art does not become the coffin for consent-
even when a 10-year-old's piercing eyes
captivates the soul of a white man.

THE IDEA OF HOME

I would quite like to understand the idea of home.
Bean Station below the mountain to Tazwell-
vast gluttonous fistfuls of untainted land
where somehow progress and government
refuse to come to some.
Back there, rattlesnakes fatter than the fingers of a god
slunk silently in brambles and brush piles,
lurking coiled up in the foliage,
fangs ready to strike the foolish intruder.

I would quite like the idea of home
if I could slam a shot of lightning-hot moonshine
strong enough to guide me muddy boot through
a place in the Bean Station holler
or along the Chattanooga River that
felt familial and defined rather than
splintered into a torn asunder abstract.
I am them, and I am Him- a reflection of
overgrown crabgrass and heaven-touching hayfields-

       I would quite like to understand the word home

instead of being stuck in the liminal looking
at where I am going and where I have been.

A LIFE JACKET CANNOT SAVE A SINKING SUNDAY

Outward vows and looking on crowd
- wedding day meant to become a husband,
but the bride's father smiling reminded me
that I will always be a supposed bastard.

The world within and without
constrained by the same hunger
for order- the faucet will not stop dripping.

Drip,

drip,

drip.

If I go down with the ship

was I suicidal
or faithful?

CAFÉ BECAUSE I LIKE THE WAY C SOUNDS

Night always comes as expected,
long and worn thin- cardboard in the rain,
often with sugar-filled spoons clanking to sweeten
cheap burnt coffee.

Teenage summers hiding barefoot in hayricks
felt defined- time then was neither
past nor future. Now, it ambiguously passes
through susurrous milk-steaming lullabies
        drowning out the bombs
and nationalism and rhetoric exploding all around:

        Even though sunflowers will soon bloom,
        I sat baptized by cheap yellow light
        as those in the café tried to forget how everything
        changed with the burning Twin Towers.

She walked in wearing happiness
like a sundress in a blizzard with
purple paint smudged down her arm

-she was my nighthawk, a familiar face-

holding lifetimes of knowing in her steady nod
to the waitress.

The city map showed 3 a.m. train rides-
but she stopped to haunt the café

- heart aflame-

resisting the rain with
lemon water and thinning brushes.
On our stools,

we were ennui totems,
dropping moments
as sacrifices to
idols of our discontent.

April is the cruelest month until May, but she
was a respite arriving in rebellious triumph with
December cold fingers tapping the cracked counter.
The night always comes as expected, again and again and again,
a villain taunting life's lack of progress.

We have been here before, her and I-
always anticipating there would be a new frame.
Each expected night had fresh light-
giving a new shadow to love,

    convincing me that passion deferred
    is a porthole view lost at sea.

RUTTED TIRE MARKS

The green lines mix
with the pine needles in hand.
A twitch of nerve causes the cardinal to flutter off.
Unfathomed thoughts topple over falling water,
as flakes drop on the tongue.
Deer tracks and rutted tire marks
make way for the evening hike.
Squirrel crackles and chirps from above,
alienation comes with a sweet autumn breath.
Each step counsels the lost moonrises.
Lethargy given over to the minnows' liturgy.
The brittle foundation of a stagnant soul
situates itself in isolation's cove.
Unpaved paths and pantheistic pews,
a morsel of High Courts in the cascading water.

MACHINE DREAMS AND PAWNED RINGS

Love has always been found in
dumpster-diving moments
more so than sonnet dishonesty.
Machine dreams and pawned rings-
these are some of our favorite things.

Look, Pumpkin, it is way out-

    I go,
        you go,
                we all go out

                one way or the other.

What has this all been about?

Mannequins refusing to dress in our parents' clothes-
cucumber water and Himalayan hikes,
a teaspoon of life never enough, engulfed by
two-tone leggings and plain t-shirts
dancing after the dinner bell chimed.

POPLARS, POPLARS, POPLARS, CAN'T YOU SEE? SOMETIMES YOUR LEAVES JUST HYPNOTIZE ME

The rustling sounds
of the poplars and oaks
soar to the Father
as a dove's feather
descends to ashes of fallen pines.

I THREW UP IN A MINIVAN BECAUSE OF A CHILD LOCK IS NOT THE PROPER NAME FOR A SONNET BUT I BET A GOTHIC TEDDY BEAR WOULD HEAD BANG TO THAT SONG

Good fortune is not needed; washed-out gravel
roads and earth explored is fortune enough-
Someone else's kitchen is still part of the world to know-
my own is a home, but does not negate the need to roam.

Rushing through a small town,
lacking know-how- the heart beats strong
like firecrackers in a tin can.
The trees have eyes, the mailboxes have ears.

Teachers taught about a globe but never how
to find the unencumbered path.
            I am sad when the pain(t) washes off my hands.

Enormous drops of pure water from mountain springs
provokes lithium salt immune mania-
do not step back into the hand of the globe; wait right here-
run, run before the disturbed wasps leave their nest.

Why go to the west when I can float east
and scale the Himalayas?
there are those her(e) now that were not there when the false
summits of Everest kept scaling into the absurdity of the sky.

A globe can never show your tsunami emotions
under a full moon's advancement.
Addled by a gyre of anxiety and excitement,
we can explore each gust through wind-dust geysers.

A festoon path around Appalachia, closed hatchback
dressers and timber trunk bedposts-
the bristles and thorns are a home, too.
Purple strobes on a rusted cigarette machine are the only

globe that can teach about the world-

that is fortune enough:

there is always a light on in Chattanooga-

maybe we should return soon.

Nights between the bridges smelt like
goth bands in minivans-
memory frails like strawberry carcasses
sunbathing in June afternoons.

I did not know you then, but I do now-

magenta acrylics basing the day for lime green excitement-
please do not leave me –
a globe is not your home, but to see five-count breaths
and crashing waves in your morning eyes is fortune enough.
Here is my cardigan, it is cold.
A globe wraps around itself, but you never have to return
unless the call back breaks the barriers of miles.

Stalemates of empty sidewalks and stop lights-
I think I have now found my father hidden within my shadow-

Neon suns sinking through sickening smells of carrion advice
given by those with teaspoon wisdom and fat-saving accounts-
a 401k is just an unimaginative soothsayer convincing us
they can see the future, and a globe is nothing more than
another man's perspective of where others can travel-

seems I stand at a stalemate:

Pulled toward chaos, toward the road,
toward the wild where things are both abandoned
and remembered without a globe- that is the lot I rolled

sludging through tobacco-stained fields
     -please do not leave when you see that is fortune enough
even if that means we will never return to our moment.

RAIN PUDDLE SALVATION

My shoes were muddied
until baptized by rain puddles,

now they are clean.

SUGAR WE'RE GOING DOWN, PICK THE RIGHT DOOR BECAUSE IT IS EITHER DEATH OR DESTRUCTION, MAYBE WE CAN JUST DROWN

Hold onto my hips,
the fish only nibble a moment,
ignore the phantom steps,
desire digests our surroundings.

Hurry out; I am shivering,
you are laughing,
my love and my disaster.
July's heat fades into our longing,
was that a footstep heard?
Time to move higher.

The rocks patterned for ascent,
your mom will never know.

Watch closely, my grip can hold,
as my neck tenses with the elevation,
you topple down to the earth's floor.

Flashbacks of forgotten names
and slip of a son's existence –
Thirty feet down,
she would not listen,
the words sit jaded as I hold on tight.

If only your vices had been void.
Bruised and battered:
your present same as your past –
an alluding to what would come.

Why did we not heed the warning?

THERE IS A PLACE WHERE THE SUN DON'T SHINE AND THE ANGELS DON'T SING, THAT AIN'T HERE WHERE YOUR EMERALDS EYES TEMPT THE NIGHT AND YOUR HAND HOLDS A MOTH

One day you will stop to hear the birds sing-
then society's blindfold will no longer lead.

A RIVER RAPID IS NOT A SUITABLE PLACE TO HIDE A MEMORY

There were tavern words and
wrapped sourdough with burnt edges
before our last day-

Kisses felt thin like cornsilk
as we walked the rails.
Succulents and thornbush folded clothes
waited for you back at the apartment-
your parents' words, too.
There are always words before the end.
Grow or go? A dead star takes years to tell its truth.

Your parents' Cuban crisis logic dressed our nights
even with your clothes bunched in the corner
as cicadas cascaded through the thrift store
box fan in the window.

'a river rapid is not a suitable place to store a memory.'

We were polemic observers of decay.
you could not sleep wearing a shirt
but loved to tell me to stop trying to swallow the sun,
apparently, there is only one.

Rooftops were our pews looking
over streetlight dots like pastors on a psilocybin pedestal.
Your manic whims became my god,
every sophist train track once had a station,
and we walked like we could find each one-
gnostic splatters splayed across our starry refusal to go home.

Wildflowers raked wanton over your hand,
it was not okay, the door shut, it was not okay-
we stayed together because you were not okay
until every door was locked stopping stranger
words from coming in.

Phantom security danced over your cheeks when a
mockingbird melodically doddled poshly on bald bark
- a cracked jar eventually leaks
but I held the wine in my open hand
until the town went dry.

You noticed the dead branches with the living-
the bark peeled back as the pros and cons
of our nights lived through another drag.

I once was three and barefoot, wobbling shoeless
across cow pastures.
You turned thirty on those rails,
running from skewed sermons musing about cold feet
in battlefields holding tightly to chapter/verse suffocations.

It is better to bastardize love than live like a glove-
earthquake shakes shook wine on your magenta blouse.
In the alarm clock glare, shirtless, you held tight, whispering,
'if the sun never rose, then the flight would not come-
maybe you should swallow the sun since there is only one.'

Surely that confirms there are always words before the end.

THE CREEK ROLLS AND MOMMA MADE DINNER ROLLS- AMEN

What is change,
from what cave does the word derive?

Down in the holler where the creek rolls,
can a man find the strength to stray
from the nature that nurtured his narcissism
that only takes from the well without refilling.

The vineyard that made the bitter wine in his emptying cup
would wilt without rain.
If to wilt is to change, then should the petals of youth
stray from the rain? Or is there wisdom in
fat plumb drops watering the roots to grow?

THERE WAS A TIME WHEN I WAS HERE

Time slows as it melts into a frozen river,
tumults of that which is happening flow into that which is gone.

I do not progress, I disintegrate-
When death comes flipping a quarter in the air
where will time go?

Life lived is a door of curiosity that decays- a nightmare alley
full of fun mirrors and twisted tales told through the dark
clothes cabinets masquerading as a body.

                    -I swear I was here-

Dreams and bones and all the pretty things
are full of meaning. Then an eschaton collapses as another star dies
and meaning droops out of the hourglass
into irrelevances, making the bubble gum popping
nights suffer from lack of definition
like they are asphyxiated moments strung out
waiting for a restart.

If time is gone once experienced, was it ever here?

I am here! I am Here!   I am here until I am not
           then scars that I left will be my testimony-
but I swear there was a time when I was here.

DONNIE DARKO'S WORMHOLE IS THE PERFECT PLACE FOR AN ENGAGEMENT

Circular reasoning presupposes the beginning as the end-
to leave is the same as coming back,
but if nature is my rabbi
then maybe there is a wormhole where time
warbles and freezes to hear the cicadas
dancing to the lightning bugs' rhythm.

My coming and going shows the hairline fractures
in high fructose conversations as the
life of the day wanes under the pressure of the coming tide.

Sealed nuclear shadows from the bombs of war
spread on the margin of understanding-
        the only cure is a fissure of ascending and descending
outside of America's broken ouroboros
to find perspective in the clouds and the valley.

I am not stuck, I am not stuck, the crow can fly and
I swear I am not stuck until I see another
sieving obligation through a mesh of meditation and Thoreau-
        destroying false summits guided by corporate shamans-
        drop your youth for the gods, kid, it is the only way to live.
I am not stuck, I swear I am not stuck, until I realize that
I allowed another to swallow the end where the new could begin.

DID YOU KNOW FISH ORGIES CAN MAKE A DOLPHIN GO DEAF

I am not, but I am.

Seasons of growth led to crooked fingers
and thumbprint smudges on the desk:
the words and empty park walks,
analogous symbols of how I am not a red canna.

In time, I looked at her, soused with
dopamine fixes- they have become less effective lately:
wine spilling out of shattered pear bottom jars.
In time, I looked at her, wanting her to be the bottom
of the jar I emptied.

I am not Barbie, but I am plastic,
a walking mold wishing to escape

  from Dramamine transience-

Gibberish scribbled is an heirloom of time gone-
chipped pencil lead swatted off the paper-
I forgot my flashlight right when it was time to go.

The forest exists, guarding the soil that hides
under the burnt tree trunks- my heart still lives
amongst the pines to prove this true.
Intent separates arson and inspiration:
I am plastic, not a red canna.

If life did not suffer change, it would be almost bearable-
cannas will wilt no matter if watered or not,
macular degeneration refuses to covet beauty-

I wilt, too- but I recognize the difference
between the flower's soul and mine.

74

The world outside the pink door proves
that I am not a red canna, poet maybe,
plastic, definitely.

It is time to turn this ship, but
a scared captain locks his door when he rests-
a man confined is a man defined.

I have never killed wearing lemon-colored gloves,
but have murdered the night when her eyes dimmed
after I halfway listened to what I thought she said
pushing warmth towards the cliff.

          -I am not, but I am:
there is just enough love in that pipe to blow out the
last ember in the spark

allowing my apology to start by admitting that
I am plastic, not a red canna.

A DARKNESS WHERE I WISH TO BE

There is never enough freedom out there,
never enough open air for the dove to dive
without falling into the cars' brown fog.

Our apocalypse eyes wait to burn the
boardwalks during dusty nights
where whiskey dreams sit on our teeth-
there was not enough freedom out there-

       but somewhere there is a darkness where I wish to be-

it leaps about as I go, it leaps about
as though it knows there is not enough freedom
on North Carolina highways or South Carolina coasts-
       do you dare come with me if I do not go back out there?

Pewter lights hang in here where no one dares
to park after night- but we are just fine if it is just you and I,
crystals in our hands and white glasses on the brim of your nose
looking into the abyss for intruders at dusk.

The swell of clouds, little worlds calling-
one more hit so we can go higher-
a match can only light a wick it touches.
Strange deadwood sounds and wrens watching
the pupil in your eyes. They know
sleep under the blood moon
       is the darkness where I wish to be.

Blackberry brambles prick my nicotine finger-
       there is life in the blood-
as I pick breakfast in the hue of humid dawn
never thinking of out there-
knowing by your sleeping side is the darkness where I wish to be.

CHACO TAN LINES, PEBBLE JAW SPEAKING, A SHOE TODAY MEANS CONFORMITY TOMORROW

Chaco feet swinging off a cliff,
Tennessee River sweetly swaying below,
bristles from apple crisp fall winds
walk gently down my skin
like the nights she ran her fingers
down my spine.

SEIZE THE DAY SNARKS AND EIFFEL TOWER DREAMS

Nights outside stolen by the factories-
we know if more minimum wage work left, there would be
       another silver spoon to burn to see the
       hollow light of the holler glowing bright-
down in the valley, the gospel moved at night
without taillights, flicking cigarette butts in the driveway.

Modeling seize the day snarks and shakes
from seizures below the underpass,
we hopped off the pier and tree-planted our feet
in the sandy shores looking towards the Eiffel Tower-
a shadow never seen- is it real if country bumpkins can never see?-
hearing the guttural growl from the
Bean Station demon that followed us
through Carolina mountains and Florida interstates.

We will be something, we have to be something.
We are, you never could say what we are.

HONKING HORNS SOUND LIKE SOMEONE SHOULD HAVE STAYED HOME AND MADE PUDDING

I went to the woods when
cascading cars and honking horns
created a misery wormhole.

There, even the barren fields are clothed
with more splendor and wisdom
than my wildest borrowed imagination-

      I go to find what the speckled forest floor
      never has thought could be lost.

A crane watches, hiding in a field of
lemon yellow creeping buttercups.
this land is his, not mine,
but here I go to shrink life.

Tree limbs stretched, yearning for the addled bay,
knowing where to go even if I need to be shown the way.

Do the trees chatter amongst themselves,
bemoaning our noise-polluting intrusion –
the human privilege of being in
land not our own?

Blooming clouds dot the crane's sky.
Song sparrows twitter during the stilled wind,
echoes bouncing through cobwebs.

Spring crickets hidden amongst the earthen hues.
notes of distant decay that
exploded into fiery hues still
shine at the edge of our
elastic cosmic expanse.

My face reflects back-
does the water share a mirror's ontology
or do I share with the intruder
when the oils from my finger seep into
the smooth barren knot surrounded
by weather-beaten cracked bark of the Slippery Elm?

Branches not made straight- seasonal liturgy,
ethereally guided, yet I straighten
my written words to ease the chaos
of not slowing down.
I do not wish to wilt between stops

when to the woods I can go-
                    I must decrease,
                    its presence must increase

and the sounds of snails sliding over rocks
must help me escape man's chaos
to see the divinity of oyster mushrooms
growing on the fallen birch
hidden in entropic order.

JUPITER EYES

Scars of shake-and-bake nights across your face-
meth momma, porkchop baking.
We burnt your pop's leather belt-

    burn, baby, burn

the moonshine burnt going down faster than his
pride when he pelted us with Bible verses
and needle-induced curses as we ran to the car-
        lost authority, lost identity, a drunken man without his belt
        loses his purchased purity.

Baptism River, bloody fist of drunk nights,
divorce papers, soured milk, and budget lucky charms-
      is the American Dream written
      on your worn-out shoes
      or skipped days from school?

They have seen it all,

    crawl along, crawl along

They have known all along.

With your Jupiter eyes and questions why
you smile at the burning belt and write on my arm.

Will you be my ghost
on our social island?

A BUG IN A DRESS IS A LADY BUG, A BUG IN MY PALM IS SCIENCE

Grass blades wet our shoe'd feet.
We walk– wandering.
Heartache and hope intermingled.
What will come of us?

Light flashed, for a moment–
meager curiosity pulls.
Whispers of the dead,
draw of the night.

Come, this way– let us see.
Maybe something,
maybe nothing is more likely,
but we will see what comes of us.

The night stills as our hands freeze.
Remember to talk plainly,
we need to hear again–
against the grain of surety.

Even though it looks lost,
focus on the unseen.
Wait, wilt, so the flowers can bloom –
the A.M. shall come.

Manic memories, morsels of fear –
all strange works steer.
The path is unkempt, dust flies,
but only for one more moment.

What will come of us?

NAMASTE, YOU FILTHY ANIMAL, NAMASTE- NOW WE ARE CLEAN

Addled, hurried-
　　　hollow.

Witch hazel branches and orange blood moon,
a world below and above-
but my mind stays on
the other side of the mountain,
Disconnection disassembles connection-
purpose in movement-
savasana waits in stillness.

　　　Where is peace?

Hollow words, hollow footsteps-
destruction yokes my out-of-breath soul
to the drive to be something other than
that which I already am-
　　　crisis orbits the horizon.

Addled, hurried- hollow man ways-

There is a here where I can hear
the purple-crested dwarf Iris
bend when the bee lands to pollinate-

　　　but why am I fixated on a there yet to come-
　　　bite the spotted red apple Adam:
　　　that which is not is better than that which is.

My body- a temple destroyed.
The sodden path trodden over- a temple destroyed.
Stopping to yoke temporal body and eternal earth- a temple healed:

　　　Namaste.

SCHRODINGER'S DAD

Father, you claimed I was not yours, even
before that strange doctor wiped off my birthmark foot.

Sex set this off like an accidental spark
in a pile of dry leaves-
neither of you asked my permission to score
the scars before the baby seat sat securely in her car-

Memories underdeveloped,
        like overexposed film
any time I want to care.

Copperhead wishes, full of ignorant fangs:
a bastard son does not paint their pater's face.

Empty, hollow- you had no right to steal the word father,
sticking me in a doll house to act out rejection
whenever you decide it is time.

I am not your son, I am your lie-
you poke and stir, trying to infect an open wound.

To be entre paises
is to wilt between being a bastard and adopted,
fat-handed child and dirty-nail adult.
Father, you are not alive, you are imagined:
forever a thief, tucked away in a plum fat emotional bruise.

I gorge your memory's ration to understand
my identity as a lie-
pulled like a frailed rubber band
trying to solve Schrodinger's dad.

A sunrise has no utility if preoccupied with why
you stay hidden in the witchy-eyed skyline,
never more than a blank wall refusing to accept paint-
I tried to remember your face,

but it was an impotent distant earthquake.

These words are not mine; they belong to a snail
that crawled through sticky mud to escape a crushing foot.
Hear the scream! Hear the scream!
Blackjack hand and whiskey gummed,
I can hear the scream of the dust sucking into the muffler
when you drove off dropping your seed in a field,
not caring that the wind would kidnap me.

I HAVE A MATCH IF YOU HAVE AN EMOTION I HAVE NOT LET DOWN

I would burn down the city to show you night-popping lights,
but you asked to run along the Ocoee River
chasing blackbirds and sounds unheard.

The echoes of your plea
bounce through the mental caverns
of unoccupied space
where I alchemize reality to fit my fear.

I would burn down the city to show you night-popping lights,
but you asked to run along the Ocoee River
chasing blackbirds and sounds unheard.

You lament being made in the image of a
distant daydream
when I fight with an assumption rather
than for the rope from the moment's sinking ship.

The moment's event horizon approaches
with abstracted words and the record needle-skimming
our favorite Further Seems Forever song-

I flee down a dark alley of assumed ideas,
trying to escape the cacophony of shadows gathered
from broken alabaster jars and given-back antique rings.

Too many tides rise while
I make you a false wall creation,
a diction all to my own-
a tornadic dichotomy of who you are
and the shadows of unadmitted fears.

DEATH DANCES, DARLING- YES THAT IS CRINGE BUT I REALLY NEED ATTENTION SINCE MY PHONE DIED

Soured coffee oil, sweat –
stagnant love on my brow.
Pill bottles opened –
searching for escapism's rescue.

Walk or trip –
sleep somberly awaits.
Turned cheek and whisky breath,
death dances, darling.

Fingernails chewed –
no one is home,
heckled henna drawings designed,
with weighty silence.

Fickleness ignored,
impatience's scratches scar.
Hollowed word shaken
you continue on.

Up, or maybe down –
direction not defined.
Yet, here I sit –
the dark ladies pawn.

Banter and curse words –
date night's misery.
Swallow, close your eyes –
goodbye is passive and sweet.

TITLES ARE SUPPOSED TO BE SHORT, BUT THIS IS A LOADED GUN MOMENT WHERE I WANT CHICKEN NUGGETS AND PASCAL THOUGHTS WITHOUT THE COMMITMENT.

At the end, days are a warm bath
with emotions like a bus crash:
An oeuvre of broken moments scattered
in spitless dust-
blind, blind, blind,
blind liturgy
words in a loop, fixated on a thought until wrung dry,
mind threatening to be a heart, not a brain:
blind, blind, blind-
please spit in the dust.

      Make some mud for my eyes.

There is a hidden door protecting naked fingers.
To leave is not enough, but sometimes all there is.

Life is a sculpture chiseled
with the hands of uncontrolled reactions and others' perspectives.

There is a door where one does not ask me to be
a grape on the vine waiting to be wine.
Splattered plaster and shards of glass
left behind to sit in a land silent as an abandoned crab shell.

A cedron tree awaits- the door is all that is mine.
Every year has a first week of September, a date to find,
the timbers in the west sit in my mind in the east.

My breath, my door, a contradiction
to a thousand half-loves and saccharine sweet lies.

Stop, people are watching!
They always say.

I know-

where is the door?

Christ wants me to be different, too-

where is the door?

In the end, it is a warm bath and
emotions like a bus crash,
maybe one day, it will be
the place I can finally drown
and Lyra can hand over the key
to the door that is only mine.

WAVES- THIS IS THE GIVING UP EFFORT COLLEGE PROFESSORS EXPECT

The waves come closer and closer-
no ravine, no flood line:
the tide will soon wipe away your footprints.

APOLOGIES WORK BETTER IN THE DARK WITH A SLOTH AND WINE

A wild delight runs into my mind when
I think I have captured who you really are,
but you sit crossed-legged, holding a heavy-eyed
wrecking ball waiting for me to stop
imagining, to start listening-
knowing I must tear up the tattered daguerreotypes
    or risk-reducing you to someone neither have met before.

A CAR CRASH SEEMS LIKE A BAD WAY TO END A FIRST DATE, BUT SOMETIMES IT IS THE ONLY WAY TO AVOID TURTLE ANARCHY AND AN AWKWARD GOODBYE

I once disappeared in Guntersville.

That is not now-

this is a down- a manic rhapsody with
a rotten arm trying to claw at a crow's caw.

I am easily found like a broken mirror after an earthquake.
For decorum's sake, I dress my face with that consistent smile
she likes so well- a whittled marionette.

Summer silhouettes shudder under
bayou sticky steps through unfamilial boardwalks:
Dracula dancing in the daytime, pennies in the pocket
every face is a refraction of where I thought I was supposed to go-

If there is a distant lighthouse, dilapidated dreams block its shine.
This is a down, she is not invited, no one is- except maybe one-

My chattering tongue feels numb and full of lies.

An urn on the mantle is my staff in the wilderness.
today I am obsessed with the whole,
watching time spin like a thimble of arsenic on my thumb-

All street sign colors remind me of her faded lipstick,
I am terrified of this thing in me- a fast-talking hurricane
of wonder- the pot boils over as a feverish gleam,
convoluted by insular metaphors.

This is a down, a holy robe of mania, not a time to
devour states like an angry God, wrung out
from the responsibilities of emotions- mish-mashed exhaustion,

the world is a doll house for the whole, not the maimed.

To be the center is to repel- that fits snug
as I live like a shrug, hanging pictures that prove that I live
better as a mannequin than a son.

This is a down, a dark holler mania-
she does not belong here,

       no one does,

            except maybe one.

THERE IS SOMETHING SINISTER TO IT

Life is not a choice; it is a must-
to know the bottom is to know it all.

There is something sinister to it
like a labyrinth of accidental encounters
until green sheets crinkle under
cooing coffee pots and clinking wine glasses-

it is memory, it is amnesia-

Etherized revelations
lying on a society's gurney
wondering if food stamps
can pay student loans-
            declaration of dependence-

Formaldehyde glances at the watch
to see embalmed 5'oclocks impose sentences
en masse for the pied Piper of
Ponzi scheme dreams.

Waves crashing against rocks weather
the edges- there is something sinister to it-
like masks at night- is it COVID or hypnosis?
Am I the psychosis? Or the raft floating freely
through blue and yellow dreams?

A smile, a chuckle, neither stays.
Acidic undertones to cryptic days
of steaming pots waiting to explode-
pressure cookers in a backpack.
Backtracked steampunk rants when rent
cannot be paid.

I never knew these things-
there is something sinister to it,
like lightening bug graveyards
next to college degrees.
Cracked jars and broken penny banks
to pay for bus fare to go home-
                I now know the bottom.
Double-wide hope looking at the glowing yonder,
tomato seeds growing,
biscuits in molasses stuck against rusted forks.
Splinters in the finger while climbing
rotting barn steps.

Vapors fade in between fingers
as scowls howl on cassette apologies.
Life's discontent is a mirror of the beginning
and the end-
                to know the bottom is to know it all.

Late-night bluff shooters- do you jump or fall?
There is something sinister to it,
the pendulum swings between
depression and transcendence-
Carnival grease on our thrift store shoes-
cemented rhetoric seeps through manic memoirs,
growing desperation acts as a microcontroller making
our steps liturgical- nuclear-marching ants-
death's serenade is a lullaby-
                death to vision,
                death to art,
                death to show we can play our part.

There is something sinister to it,
life is a must, not a choice,
                and to know the bottom is to know
                that this is all.

96

A BUSHEL OF OKRA FRIED WITH CORNBREAD BATTER MAKES A HEARTBROKEN BOY WEEP A LITTLE LESS WHEN WATCHING BOY MEETS WORLD

Many paths remain undisturbed, and
more cobbled creek bottoms are yet to be crossed.
Distant oceans and lands unexplored
stayed foreign to me, stuck between okra bushes and
urn collections.

Only on fertile tomato soil-
land left in deeds-
have my feet softly treaded,
fearing that my body will know
the bottom of those oceans before
the heights of the Himalayas:
the mind addling unknown
has so far stopped my mud-bitten ankles
from crossing foreign shores.

LOOK, THIS MIGHT BE A POEM, IT MIGHT BE THE PLEA, EITHER WAY AT LEAST WE ARE HERE TOGETHER

Does society want diversity
or relevance?

Diversity takes sacrifice-
      quick to listen.

Relevance takes from all-
      quick to speak.

DAL IN NEPAL TASTES BETTER THAN IN AMERICA BECAUSE WHAT IS FINE DINING OTHER THAN POMP AND CIRCUMSTANCE

A handful of earth from
Nepal's unending mountains
is still earth when
mixed with Tennessee red clay.

THIS IS A TITLE ABOUT A POEM THAT TALKS ABOUT POETRY SO IT NEEDS A TITLE AND THIS IS THE BEST I CAN DO

A good poem is a riverside walk with nowhere to be,
people around, no one there- ontologically inclusive:
pause, breathe.

It is the sun slowly sloping under the mountains,
giving way to crescent moon waves.

A good poem interests humankind permanently as an abstract
and contradiction- both deconstruction and construction holding
opposing tensions.

It is not subject to reason but walks in the shadows of every reason
before haunted by the stutters that reveal the cracked veneer.

A good poem is life had, life lost, crumbling cornbread falling to the
ground and cast-iron skillets rusted after an earthquake:
pause, breathe.

It is a meditation, a moment of inquiry and disdain,
droplets of acid rain on a society that seethes with consumerism.

A good poem is now, it is then, and is flummoxed by
surviving potholed roads of forgotten cities where the pen has been.

It is knowing the difference between who and how, defining
boundaries, creating space- an invitation and warning:

A good poem is...
pause, breathe.

It is life offered, life taken, knowing there are no good and bad
poems: only connection or disconnection.

www.ingramcontent.com/pod-product-compliance
Lightning Source LLC
Chambersburg PA
CBHW011231120626
46549CB00008B/3222